In My Own Words

The Diary of
JOSEPH PLUMB MARTIN,
a Revolutionary War Soldier

edited by Connie and Peter Roop

illustrations and maps by Laszlo Kubinyi

BENCHMARK BOOKS

MARSHALL CAVENDISH
NEW YORK

ACKNOWLEDGMENT
With thanks and appreciation to the Wisconsin State Historical Society,
Madison, Wisconsin, for providing access to Joseph Plumb Martin's
rare and valuable volume

For our Canadian readers, and any others who use the metric system,
here is a quick conversion table to help you with the weights and
measures used in this book.

Distance
1 mile = 1.6 kilometers
1 rod = 5.5 yards
1 yard = 0.9 meters
1 foot = 30.48 centimeters

Volume
1 gill = ½ cup
1 cup = 237 milliliters
1 tablespoon = 14.8 milliliters

Weight
1 pound = 453.59 grams

Benchmark Books
Marshall Cavendish Corporation
99 White Plains Road
Tarrytown, New York 10591-9001
Illustrations and maps copyright © 2001 by Marshall Cavendish Corp.
Copyright © 2001 by Connie and Peter Roop

Library of Congress Cataloging-in-Publication Data
Martin, Joseph Plumb, 1760-1850.
In my own words: the diary of Joseph Plumb Martin, a Revolutionary War soldier / edited
by Connie Roop and Peter Roop.
     p.   cm—(In my own words)
Includes bibliographical references and index.
Summary: The diary of a young Connecticut farmer, who fought against the British in
the Revolutionary War.
ISBN 0-7614-1014-7(lib.bdg.)
1. Martin, Joseph Plumb, 1760-1850—Juvenile literature. 2. United
States—History—Revolution, 1775-1783—Personal narratives—Juvenile literature.
3. Soldiers—United States—Diaries—Juvenile literature. [Martin, Joseph Plumb,
1760-1850. 2. Soldiers. 3. United States—History—Revolution, 1775-1783—Personal
narratives. 4. Diaries.] I. Roop,Connie. II. Roop, Peter. III. Title. IV. In my own words
(Benchmark Books (Firm))
E275 .M38   2000   973.3'092—dc21   99-087430

Printed in Hong Kong
1   3   5   6   4   2

For Father,
whose family fought in the Revolutionary War

Martin's Book

A

NARRATIVE

OF SOME OF THE

ADVENTURES, DANGERS AND SUFFERINGS

OF A

REVOLUTIONARY SOLDIER;

INTERSPERSED WITH

ANECDOTES OF INCIDENTS THAT OCCURRED WITHIN HIS
OWN OBSERVATION.

WRITTEN BY HIMSELF.

" Long sleepless nights in heavy arms I've stood;
" And spent laborious days in dust and blood."
POPE'S HOMER.

HALLOWELL:

PRINTED BY GLAZIER, MASTERS & CO.

No. 1, Kennebec-Row.

1830.

INTRODUCTION

George Washington, Patrick Henry, Thomas Jefferson, Benjamin Franklin, Samuel Adams, Paul Revere . . . the names ring out like the Liberty Bell. Famous men in fateful times.

But have you ever thought about the thousands of other patriots, the "little" people—the farmers, shopkeepers, clerks, fishers, sailors—who left their comfortable homes and took up arms to fight for freedom? What were their lives like as they struggled with hunger, ached with weariness, fought boredom, and faced death as soldiers in the Revolutionary War?

For most, their names and deeds are lost to history, for they kept no record of their trials and triumphs.

Fortunately for us, a soldier named Joseph Plumb Martin decided to share his adventures and misadventures with his family. At age seventy he wrote a journal of his war years, entitled *A Narrative of Some of the Adventures, Dangers and Sufferings of a Revolutionary War Soldier, Written by Himself.*

Martin was born and raised in the New England colonies. When the war began in 1775, he was too young and, at first, reluctant to fight. With trepidation, he signed up at the age of fifteen, on July 16, 1776. Martin spent the next six months as a private in the army. When his enlistment time expired, he returned home. But after a winter of ease, he enlisted again, this time for the duration of the war.

When we first read Martin's story, we were struck by his personality—his special voice, sense of humor, and adventurous spirit. We shared the miseries of camp life from rain to cold, from hunger to boredom. We ran breathless with him as he escaped capture. We held steady as he aimed his musket to shoot an enemy. We felt the bone-weariness of digging trenches or marching all night. Through his words, we felt as if we were experiencing the Revolutionary War firsthand.

This, then, is Martin's own account of his life as a soldier. As he said, "Have patience just to hear me out. I'll tell you what I've been about."

—Connie and Peter Roop
Appleton, Wisconsin

The Diary of Joseph Plumb Martin,

Telling of the Adventures, Dangers, and Sufferings of a Revolutionary War Soldier

My Early Days

The heroes of all Histories, Narratives, Adventures, Novels, and Romances have ancestors. My father was the son of a "substantial New England farmer," as we Yankees say. Grandfather farmed in the colony, but now state, of Connecticut. My mother was a farmer's daughter. Her native place was in the county of New Haven, in the same state. By the time I was born, in 1760, my parents resided in Berkshire County, Massachusetts.

I was born on Thanksgiving Day, which is celebrated with good cheer. When I was seven years old, I was sent to live in Connecticut with my mother's father. There I lived until the army became my home.

A Soldier? Not I!

Time passed smoothly for me till 1774 arrived, when the smell of war began to be pretty strong. I determined to have no hand in it, happen when it might. I felt myself to be a real coward. What! Venture my carcass where bullets fly? That will never do. Stay at home out of harm's way, thought I.

But the pinch of game had not arrived yet. I had seen nothing of war affairs and was a poor judge of such matters.

The winter of this year passed without any frightened alarms. The spring of 1775 arrived. Expectations of some fatal event filled the minds of most of the people throughout the country.

I Change My Mind

I was ploughing a field on April 21st, 1775, when all of a sudden the bells fell to ringing. Three guns were repeatedly fired in the village.

I set off to see what the commotion was. I found most men together. Soldiers for Boston were needed. (I had not known of the recent events at Concord, when shots were exchanged for the first time. We Americans won this first encounter.)

A dollar deposited upon the drumhead was taken up by someone as soon as placed there. The holder's name was taken, and he was enrolled

I WAS PLOUGHING A FIELD ON APRIL 21ST, 1775, WHEN ALL OF A SUDDEN
THE BELLS FELL TO RINGING.

with orders to equip himself as quick as possible. My spirits revived at the sight of the money offered. The seeds of courage began to sprout.

O, if I were but old enough to put myself forward, I would be in the possession of one dollar, the dangers of war notwithstanding.

I durst not put myself up for a soldier for fear of being refused. That would have quite upset all the courage I had drawn forth.

What was I to do? I was as earnest now to be called a soldier as I had been a year before not to be called one.

The War

During the following winter I collected pretty correct ideas of the contest between this country and the mother country, and I became as warm a patriot as the best of them. As the war was being waged, I felt more anxious than ever to be called a defender of my country.

Soldiers were enlisting for a year's service. I did not like that. It was too long a time for me at first trial. I wished only to take a priming before I took upon myself the whole coat of paint of a soldier.

I Become a Soldier

In the month of June 1776 orders came to enlist men for only six months. This suited me better.

One evening I went off with full determination to enlist at all hazards. At the meeting place enlisting orders were presented to me. I took up the pen and loaded it with the fatal charge. I made several imitations of writing my name, but took care not to touch the paper with the pen. Someone leaning over my shoulder gave my hand a stroke which caused the pen to make a woeful scratch on the paper.

"O, he has enlisted," said the man. "He has made his mark. He is fast enough now."

Well, thought I, I may as well go through the business now as not. So I wrote my name.

And I was a soldier! I had obtained my heart's desire. Now it was my business to prove myself equal to the profession.

To be short, I went with several soldiers on board a sloop bound for New York. We marched into the city and joined the rest of the regiment already there.

The Campaign of 1776

My First Fight

One day an officer ordered us to march to Long Island, the British having landed a force there. I got myself ready as soon as possible. I went to the top of a house, where I had a full view of that part of the Island. I saw the smoke of the field artillery. The horrors of battle presented themselves to my mind in all of their hideousness. I must come to it now, I told myself.

We took a ferry and landed at Brooklyn, where we began to meet wounded men. Some with broken arms, some with broken legs, and some with broken heads. The sight of these made me think of home. Would I live to see it?

We marched a short distance, when we halted to refresh ourselves. Whether we had any other victuals besides hard bread I do not remember. I do remember my gnawing at the bread.

> victuals
> (VIH tuls)
> supplies
> of food

It was hard enough to break the teeth of a rat.

The Americans and British were warmly engaged within sight of us. What were the feelings of most or all of the young soldiers at this time, I know not, but I know what were mine: I will do my duty as well as I am able and leave the event with Providence.

We were called upon to fall in and proceed. The enemy had driven our men into a creek. They poured grapeshot into them like a shower of hail. Many men were killed in the creek. More were drowned. We went into the water later and took out corpses and guns sunk in the mud.

Our regiment lay on the ground all night. The next afternoon we had a considerable tight scratch with an equal number of British. Our men drove the British back.

The enemy were reinforced and drove us back. We attacked again. The English were soon routed. We dared not follow them for fear of falling into a snare as the whole British army was near. We did not have anyone killed out-right. Several were severely wounded. Some, I believe, mortally.

I came through my first battle tired but

unharmed. I do not know what damage my shots did, if any.

The Battle of Kip's Bay

Our regiment marched to Kip's Bay. One evening we heard a heavy cannonade at New York. Before dark we saw four enemy ships coming up the East River. At daybreak, the first thing that "saluted our eyes" were the four ships at anchor. They lay within musket shot of us.

What is the meaning of this, thought I? The British appeared very busy on shipboard. We lay still and showed our good breeding by not interfering with them, as they were strangers. We knew not but they were bashful.

As soon as it was fairly light, we saw their boats coming out of a creek on the Long Island side filled with British soldiers. When they came to the edge of the tide, they formed their boats in a line. They added to their forces from the island until they appeared like a large clover field in full bloom.

It was a Sabbath morning, the day on which the British always employed their deviltry if possible. They said they had the prayers of the church on

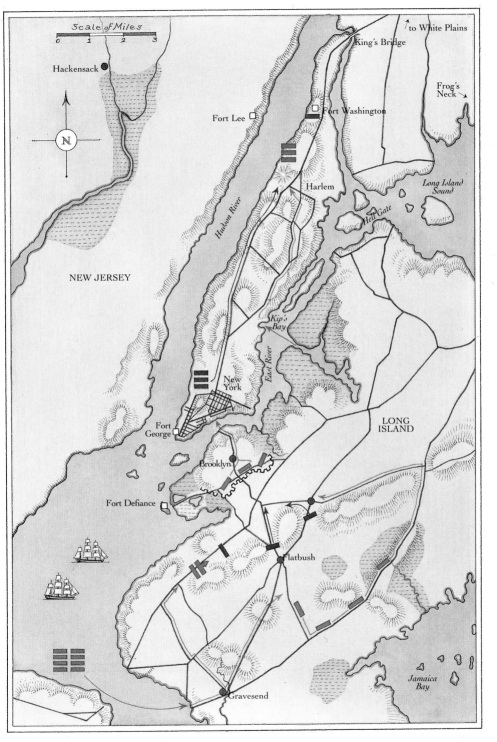

BRITISH ■ AND AMERICAN ■ POSITIONS IN NEW YORK

that day. We lay very quiet in our ditch waiting their motions, till the sun was an hour high. We heard a cannonade at the city, but our attention was drawn toward our own guests. They being a little dilatory in their operations, I stepped into an old warehouse and sat down upon a stool.

All of a sudden there came a peal of thunder from the British ships that I thought my head would go with the sound. I made a frog's leap for the ditch and lay as still as I possibly could. I began to consider which part of my carcass was to go first.

dilatory
tardy, slow

The British played their parts well. Indeed, they had nothing to hinder them. We kept our lines till they were almost upon us. Our officers, seeing we must be entirely exposed to the rake of their guns, gave the order to leave the lines.

We Retreat

In retreating we crossed level ground fifty rods wide. We were exposed to the whole of the enemy's fire. They gave it to us in prime order. The grapeshot flew merrily, which quickened our motions. When I had gotten out of reach of their combustibles, I found myself in company of a neighbor of mine when at home.

We had not gone far before we saw a party of men, hurrying in the same direction as ourselves. We endeavored hard to overtake them, but on approaching found they were not of our way of thinking. They were Hessians! We immediately altered our course and took the main road leading to King's Bridge.

We had not been long on this road before we saw another party whom we knew to be Americans. Just as we overtook them, they were fired upon by a party of British from a cornfield. All was immediately in confusion again.

The enemy's party was small, but our people were all militia. The demons of fear and disorder took full possession of all and everything that day. The militiamen did not tarry to let the grass grow under their feet. When I came to the spot where the Americans had been fired upon, I saw that the ground was covered with arms, knapsacks, staves, coats, hats, old oil flasks.

We had to advance slowly, for my comrade was now so overcome by heat, hunger, and fatigue that he became suddenly and violently sick. While I stopped to assist in constructing a litter [stretcher] for a wounded man, my sick

Hessians

The American War of Independence was
not popular in Britain. A number of British
supported the colonists' right to be free.
Others did not want to be at war with their
cousins across the sea. Also, the war was a
great distance away, some three thousand
miles. As a result, the government of King
George III had difficulty finding soldiers.
To increase British ranks, the king turned
to mercenaries—soldiers who were paid to
fight—from the state of Hesse, in what is
now Germany.

Although they were paid by Great
Britain, the Hessians wore their own
uniforms. Some thirty thousand Hessians
served in the British army. Many enjoyed
America so much that they settled here and
became citizens after the war ended.

companion, growing impatient, moved on.

We proceeded a short distance before we found
our retreat cut off by the enemy.

I quitted the road and went into the fields. There happened to be a small boggy spot of land covered with low bushes and weeds. Squatting down, I concealed myself from the enemy. Several British came so near I could see the buttons on their clothes. They withdrew and left the coast clear for me again.

I Find My Friend

I came out and went on. What had become of my comrade and the rest of my companions I knew not. I kept my friend's musket. I was unwilling to leave it for it was his own property and I knew he valued it highly. I had, though, enough to do to take care of my own concerns.

It was exceedingly hot, and I was faint, having slept very little the preceding night. Nor had I eaten a mouthful of victuals for more than twenty-four hours.

I waddled on as well and as fast as I could. I soon came to a number of men at a small brook where they had stopped to drink and rest. Leaving them, I went on alone again. I passed through a gap in a fence. Here I found a number of men resting under the trees. The first I saw was my sick

The Militia

Before the War of Independence there was
no American army. There was only the
British army. Each colony had a militia to
help the British army. A militia was not a
professional army. Instead, it was an organized group of soldiers who fought only
when called upon, usually at a moment's
notice. These soldiers were nicknamed the
"minutemen," because they could assemble
their weapons and supplies quickly. The
militia had no regular uniforms, but many
minutemen wore a hunting shirt, brown or
gray breeches, and a three-cornered hat.
While not as highly organized as the British
army, the American minutemen proved
their equal in many battles throughout
the war.

friend. I was exceedingly glad to find him, for I
had little hope of ever seeing him again. He was
sitting near the fence with his head between his

knees. I tapped him on the shoulder and asked him to go with me.

"No," he said. "I must die here."

I argued the case with him, but to no purpose. He insisted upon dying there. At length with more persuasion and some force, I succeeded in getting him upon his feet and moving.

At just that instant a considerable shower of rain wet us to the skin, we being very thinly clad. We moved forward and came to where our people had begun to make a stand. They had three field pieces fitted for action in case the British came on.

We went on a little when we overtook another man belonging to our company. He had been refreshing himself with bread and dry salt fish and was putting the fragments into his knapsack. I longed for a bite, but felt too bashful to ask him. He was too thoughtless or stingy to offer it.

We had not gone far when we came up with our regiment, resting themselves on the cold ground. Our companions rejoiced to see us, thinking we were killed or prisoners. I was sincerely glad to see them.

We were the last who came up, all the others missing were either killed or taken prisoners.

The next day the enemy followed us "hard up" and were advancing through a field. We let them advance until they arrived at a fence. Then we arose and poured a volley upon them. How many of the enemy were killed and wounded could not be known. The British were as careful as Indians to conceal their losses. There were doubtless some killed. I counted nineteen ball holes through a single rail of the fence at which the enemy were standing when the action began.

The British retreated. Our people advanced into the field. The action became warm.

We kept them retreating until they found shelter under the cannons of their ships in the river. We remained on the battleground till sunset, expecting them to attack. They showed no such inclination.

Our men were fatigued and faint, having had nothing to eat for forty-eight hours. One man complained of being hungry. A colonel, putting his hand into his coat pocket, took out an ear of Indian corn burnt as black as a coal. "Here," he said to the man. "Learn to be a soldier. Eat this."

We returned to camp on the same ground we had occupied previously. Some of our men had obtained beef. They were broiling it on sticks 'round blazing fires made of dry chestnut fence rails. The meat was as black as a coal on the outside and as raw on the inside is if it had not been near the fire. I helped myself to a feast of this raw beef, without bread or salt.

Hardships Endured

We remained here until October without anything happening, excepting starvation. That had become a secondary matter. Hard duty and nakedness were the prime evils. It now began to be cool weather, especially at night. To lie every night on the cold and often wet ground without a blanket and with nothing but thin summer clothing was tedious. In the morning the ground was as white as snow with frost. Or perhaps it would rain all night like a flood. All we could do was lie down, take our musket in our arms, place the lock between our thighs, and "weather it out."

The British landed at Frog's Neck and threatened to cut us off. We were ordered to leave. We crossed King's Bridge and directed our course to White Plains.

We encamped along the way, keeping up the old system of starving. A sheep's head I begged off the butchers was all I had for three days. One day I rambled in the woods and fields to find something to satisfy the cravings of nature. I ate a considerable quantity of chestnuts.

We arrived at White Plains to find the troops parading. The British were advancing. We packed our things, which was easily done for we had but a trifle to pack, and fell into ranks. Before we were ready to march, the battle had begun. Our regiment marched off, crossed a stream, and formed behind a stone wall and waited the approach of the enemy.

We Fight Again

The enemy made their appearance in our neighborhood. A party of Hessians and English took possession of an orchard. They would advance so far as to just show themselves, fire, and fall back and reload their muskets. Our chance was, soon as they fired, to aim at the flashes of their guns. We engaged in this for a time, when, finding ourselves flanked and in danger of being surrounded, we made a hasty retreat.

We lost in killed and wounded a considerable number. One man in our company said, "Now I

OUR CHANCE WAS, SOON AS THEY FIRED, TO AIM AT THE FLASHES OF THEIR GUNS.

am going out in the field to be killed." He was shot dead. I never saw a man so possessed with the idea of mishap as he. We fell back a little and made a stand.

We did not come in contact with the enemy again that day. At night we fell back to camp. The British took possession of a hill overlooking us. They had field artillery and entertained us with their music all the evening. We entrenched ourselves where we lay, expecting another attack.

I Am Ill but Become a Nurse

During the night we remained in our trenches. Where I happened to be stationed, the water was nearly over my shoes by morning. Many of us took violent colds. I felt the ill effects and was the next day sent back to the baggage train to get well again.

I was not alone in my misery. I had the canopy of heaven for my hospital, the ground for my hammock. I found a spot where the dry leaves had collected and made up a bed and nestled in it, having no other friend present but the sun to smile upon me. I had nothing to eat or drink, not even water. In the evening a messmate found me and brought me boiled hog's flesh and turnips without bread or salt. I could not eat it. He gave the best he had to give and had to steal that, poor fellow. Necessity drove him to stealing to satisfy the cravings of his hunger as well as to assist a fellow sufferer.

The British soon passed into New Jersey. We fell back. Our sick were sent to Connecticut to recruit more soldiers, and I was sent with them as a nurse.

I had eight sick soldiers. All they needed was a cook and something for a cook to exercise his functions on. The inhabitants here were all Tories.

Tories

Tories were Americans who sided with the British during the war. They refused to fight against their "mother country." As a result, many Tories suffered at the hands of American soldiers. Some Tories remained in the United States during the war, but many fled to Canada or went back to Great Britain. Most Tories lost property and valuables during and after the war.

One old lady, of whom I got milk, lectured on my opposition to good King George. She said the British soldiers would make us fly like pigeons. My patients would not use her milk for fear of her poisoning it. I was not afraid of her.

We celebrated Thanksgiving while we were here. Our men acquired a fine roasting pig and some pies from the local people. Of these we made an excellent Thanksgiving dinner, the best meal I had eaten since I left my grandsire's table.

My First Campaign Ends

I was discharged on the twenty-fifth day of December, my term of service having expired. I set off for my good old grandsire's, where I arrived two days later. I found my friends alive and well. They appeared to be glad to see me. I was *really* glad to see them.

I had learned something of a soldier's life, enough to keep me at home for the future. The reader will find, though, if he has the patience to follow me longer, that the ease of a winter spent at home caused me to alter my mind.

The Campaign of 1777

I Am Again a Soldier

The spring of 1777 arrived. To my surprise,
I began to think about the army again. In April,
as the weather warmed, young men began to
enlist. Orders were out for enlisting men for
three years, or for the duration of the war. The
people's opinion was the war would not continue
three years.

The inhabitants of each town were put into
squads according to their property. Each squad
furnished a man for the army. One of these
squads attacked me front, rear, and flank. I
thought I might as well get as much for my skin
as I could. I told them I would go for them and
fixed the day I would clinch the bargain.

That day, which was a muster day for the
militia, soon arrived. I went to the parade
ground, where all was liveliness. My execution
was come. I put my name to the enlisting papers

for the last time. I enlisted for the war's duration. The men gave me what they agreed. I had become the scapegoat for them.

I was again a soldier!

Death at Danbury

At this time, the British landed in Connecticut, marched twenty miles into the country, and burnt Danbury with all of its stores. They had made considerable progress to safety before the Americans came up. Our side had some severe scratches with them. Killed some, wounded some, took some prisoners. The rest reached their ships, embarked, and cleared out for New York, where they arrived much gratified by the mischief they had done.

My company, meanwhile, marched to Newtown. Here we drew our arms and equipments. Uncle Sam was careful to supply us with these articles, even if he could not give us anything to eat, drink, or wear.

We went on to Danbury, where I saw the devastation caused by the British. The town had been laid in ashes. A number of inhabitants had been murdered and cast into the burning houses. Some people endeavored to look for the burnt bones of their relatives among the rubbish of their demolished houses. The streets were flooded by the fat which ran from the barrels of pork burnt by the enemy.

We stayed a short time before marching to Old Orchard. There we were tormented by whippoorwills. A potent enemy! says the reader. Well, a potent enemy they were, at night. They began their imposing music at twilight and continued until eleven o'clock and commenced again at dawn. No man could get a wink of sleep during the serenade, which in the short nights of May seemed the whole of the night.

I Am Inoculated

I was ordered with four hundred others to be inoculated with smallpox. We received the infection and I had the smallpox favorably as did the rest. We lost none.

I left the hospital on the sixteenth day after being inoculated and joined my regiment. I was attacked with severe dysentery and broke out all over with boils. Eleven at one time appeared on my arm, each as big as half a hen's egg.

Smallpox Inoculation

Smallpox was a deadly disease that killed many colonists and soldiers. It spread rapidly among people who lived close together, such as soldiers and city dwellers. Its victims had high fevers, chills, headaches, and terrible pimples that produced scars. General Washington was very concerned about it. "We should have more to dread from it than from the Sword of the Enemy," he wrote.

Washington ordered that his troops be inoculated. They would be given a very small dose of the disease so that they could build an immunity to it. Inoculation, however, was very new at this time. Many soldiers were reluctant to undergo the treatment, which meant either becoming sick with a mild case of the pox (and becoming immune to it) or actually getting the disease and possibly dying.

In June I was ordered to King's Bridge in New York. Upon the march (which was very fatiguing, it being exceeding hot) we halted to rest. I went to a house, hoping to get something to eat. The woman of the house had been churning, and I asked her for a drink of buttermilk. She told me to drink as much as I pleased. I drank as much as I could swallow. I returned and drank again. I could never before relish buttermilk, but the extreme hunger at this time gave it a new relish. "A full belly loatheth a honeycomb, but to the hungry soul every bitter thing is sweet."

My Accident

We were on a night march advancing toward the enemy when there came a heavy thunder-shower. We were ordered into barns nearby. I thought to get a nap, but hardly had I sunk into slumber when we were discovered by the enemy. Three thousand Hessians were advancing upon us.

We hurried, the shower being at its height. We marched across fields and fences, pastures and brooks, swamps and ravines, a distance of three miles. We then stationed ourselves upon a ledge of rocks. Here we waited till the sun was two hours high. But no one coming to visit us, we marched off and left the enemy to do the same.

An accident happened next that caused me

much trouble and pain. We were ordered to take boats. Wishing to be the first in the boat, I ran to the wharf and jumped into it. There was an oar lying on the bottom of the boat. I alighted on it with my right foot, which bore the whole weight of my body. The oar rolled and turned my foot so much that it lay nearly in a right angle with my leg. When we reached our destination, I was obliged to hop on one foot for five miles to camp. It was late when I arrived at camp, and it was a long time before my foot got well and strong again.

We Fight in Pennsylvania and Lose

Our troops marched to join the main army in Pennsylvania. One evening we marched toward Philadelphia. We concluded something serious was in the wind. We marched slowly all night.

At daybreak our advanced guard and the British outposts came in contact. The curs began to bark first, then the bulldogs. We saw the enemy drawn up behind a rail fence. We formed a line and advanced. Our orders were not to fire until we saw their buttons.

They fell back. We advanced. They were driven

through their camp. They left kettles on fires in which their breakfast was cooking. Garments lay on the ground which the owners had not time to put on.

Affairs went well. The enemy retreated until our first division had expended its ammunition. Some men yelled that their ammunition was spent. The enemy were so near they overheard them and made a stand. Our people retreated. This resulted in the rout of the whole American army.

I traveled the rest of the day, after marching all the day and night before and fighting all morning. I was tormented with thirst, fighting being warm work. After the retreat I found ample means to satisfy my thirst. I could drink at the brook, but I could not bite at the bank.

I never wanted to run, when I was forced to run, further than to be beyond the enemy's shot. After that I had no more fear of their over-taking me than I should have had of an army of lobsters.

Our army collected again and the men recovered from their panic. We marched, starving and freezing, until we camped at White Marsh, twelve miles north of Philadelphia.

Our regiment was ordered to defend Fort Mifflin on Mud Island on the Delaware River, below Philadelphia.

Here I endured hardships sufficient to kill half a dozen horses. Let the reader consider for a moment and he will be satisfied if not sickened. In cold November, without provisions, without clothing, I had not a scrap of shoes or stockings to my feet or legs. In this condition we had to endure a siege in such a place that was appalling in the highest degree. I will give the reader a short description of the pen that I was confined in. Confined I was, for it was next to impossible to have gotten away.

Mud Island was a mud flat in the Delaware River. A ditch and dike were built around the fort. On the eastern side was a zigzag stone wall. On the western side was a row of barracks half the length of the fort. In front of the barracks were parade grounds and walks. The rest of the ground was soft mud. I have seen enemy's shells fall upon the mud and sink so low that their report could not be heard when they burst. I have felt the tremulous motion of the earth when they did. If they burst near the surface, they threw mud fifty feet in the air.

On the opposite side of the water, the British had erected five batteries with six heavy guns in each one and a bomb battery with three long mortars in it. They had another battery of six guns up the river.

This is the place which I was destined, with a few others, to defend against whatever force, land or marine, the enemy might see fit to bring against it.

We Are Attacked

The first attempt the British made against us was by the *Augusta*, a sixty-four-gun ship. As soon as she was discovered in the morning, we plied her so well with hot shot that she was soon in flames. Boats were sent to her assistance. Our shot proving too hot for them, they left her to her fate. She blew up with an explosion which seemed to shake the earth to its center, leaving smoke like a thundercloud for an hour. A twenty-gun ship which came to her rescue shared her fate soon after.

Nothing protected us from the enemy's guns across the way except a wall of old timber laid up

SHE BLEW UP WITH AN EXPLOSION WHICH SEEMED TO SHAKE THE EARTH
TO ITS CENTER.

in lines and filled between with mud and dirt. During the day the British batteries would nearly level our works. At night we were, like beavers, obliged to repair our dams. Each time the enemy fired their guns, our sentinels would cry, "A shot!" Upon hearing the warning everyone endeavored to take care of himself. Yet the British fire would ever and anon cut up some of us.

It was utterly impossible to lie down to get any rest or sleep on account of the mud, even if the enemy's shot would have suffered us to do so. Some men, overcome with fatigue and want of sleep, would slip away into the barracks to catch a nap of sleep. It seldom happened they all came out alive. I was in this fort a fortnight and can say I never lay down to sleep a minute in all that time.

The British knew the situation as well as we did. Their point-blank shot would not reach us hidden behind our wall, so they threw elevated grapeshot from their mortar. The grapeshot came down like a shower of hail about our ears.

We had a thirty-two-pound cannon, but had not a single cannonball for it. The British had the same kind of cannon. Our officers offered a gill of rum for each shot fired from their cannon that our soldiers could get. I saw fifty men standing on the parade ground waiting for the coming of the shot, which would often be seized before its motion had ceased. It was then conveyed to our gun to be sent back to its former owners.

We Burn Fort Mifflin

We continued here suffering cold, hunger, and other miseries till the 14th of November. At dawn, we discovered six ships and opened our batteries upon them. The enemy began firing upon us. There was music indeed. We were ordered to defend to the last extreme, as it was expected the British would land under the fire of their cannon and storm the fort. The cannonade was severe. Six sixty-gun ships, a thirty-six-gun frigate, a twenty-four-gun ship, and the other batteries added, all playing at once upon our poor little fort, if fort it might be called.

The fire was incessant. The cannonade continued without interruption throughout the day. Nearly every gun in the fort was silenced by midday. Our men were cut up like cornstalks.

As soon as it was dark, we made preparations for evacuating the fort and escaping to New

Jersey. The fort was as completely ploughed as a field. The buildings were in broken fragments. The guns dismounted. How many of the garrison were sent to the world of spirits, I knew not. If ever destruction was complete, it was here.

I was left with eighty men to burn all that was left. The enemy were so close I heard one say, "We will give it to the rebels in the morning."

I thought, "The rebels will show you a trick. They will go off and leave you."

I went to the river to find one of my mess-mates. I found him, indeed, lying in a long line of dead men who had been brought out of the fort to be conveyed to the mainland, to have the last honors conferred upon them that it was in our power to give. Poor young men!

I returned to the fort and set fire to everything that would burn. Before we could set off in our boats, the buildings in the fort were completely in flames. They threw such a light that our escape was as plainly seen by the British as though it had been broad day. Their whole fire directed at us. Our boats were thrown almost out of the water. The shot and water flew merrily. By the assistance of a kind Providence we escaped without injury and landed, after midnight, on the Jersey shore.

We marched deep into the pine woods. I wrapped myself in my blanket, lay down on some leaves, and fell asleep. When I awoke, it was past noon. That was the first sound sleep I had had in a fortnight. I was as crazy as a goose shot through the head.

We had left our American flag flying when we retreated from the island. The enemy did not take possession of the fort until late in the morning.

Here ends the account of as hard and fatiguing a job as occurred during the Revolutionary War.

Thomas Paine, speaking of the siege, says, "They had nothing but their bravery and good conduct to cover them." He spoke the truth. I was at the siege of Yorktown [in 1781, the last major battle of the Revolutionary War]. The hardships there were no more to be compared with this than the sting of a bee is to the bite of a rattlesnake. Little notice has been taken of our defense of Fort Mifflin as there was no Washington, Putnam, or Wayne there. Had there been, the affair would have been extolled to the skies. Great men get great praise. Little men, nothing. It was always so and always will be.

extol
to praise highly

Valley Forge

We crossed the Schuylkill River on a cold, rainy, snowy night upon a bridge of wagons set end to end and joined together by boards. We settled down in camp. While we lay there a Continental Thanksgiving was ordered by Congress. (The army had all the cause in the world to be thankful; if we were not well off, at least we were no worse.)

We had had nothing to eat for two days previous except what the fields and forest afforded us. But we must now have what Congress ordered, a sumptuous Thanksgiving to close the year of high living. Our country, ever mindful of its suffering army, opened her sympathizing heart so wide as to give us something to make the world stare. And what do you think it was, reader? Guess. You cannot guess? I will tell you. Our country gave each and every man half a gill of rice and a tablespoon of vinegar!

The army was now not only starved but naked. The greatest part were shirtless and barefoot. They lacked blankets. I found a piece of raw cowhide and made myself a pair of moccasins. It was this or go barefoot, as hundreds of my companions had to, till they might be tracked by

WE CROSSED THE SCHUYLKILL RIVER ON A COLD, RAINY, SNOWY NIGHT UPON A BRIDGE OF WAGONS.

their blood upon the rough frozen ground.

We marched toward Valley Forge and arrived there before Christmas. Our prospect was dreary. In our miserable condition we had to go into the wild woods and build temporary habitations. Had there fallen deep snows or heavy rainstorms, the whole army would inevitably have perished. Had the enemy, strong and well provided as he was, thought fit to pursue us, our poor emaciated carcasses would have strewed the plain. A kind and holy Providence took better care of us than did our country in whose service we were wearing away our lives.

I am not writing fiction. All are sober realities.

We next marched two days to Milltown, which was to be our quarters for the winter. We were put into a house and furnished with rations of wholesome beef and flour taken from the inhabitants nearby. We built berths for ourselves to sleep in and filled them with straw and felt as happy as any other pigs that were no better off than ourselves.

Now having got into winter quarters, I shall here end my account of my second campaign.

The Campaign of 1778

Foraging for Food

There is no end of duty in the army. There is no going home and spending the winter season among friends. It is one constant drill, summer and winter. Like an old horse in a mill, it is a continual routine.

With a small group of men, I was ordered to leave our quarters to go on foraging duty. This meant we would roam through the countryside for many weeks seeking food for the army. I was employed in this duty from Christmas until the latter part of April. I shall not relate all the transactions that passed while procuring provisions from the inhabitants, as these would swell my narrative to too large a size. I will instead give the reader a brief account of my movements.

We fared much better than I had ever done in the army before, or ever did afterward. We had some very good provisions all winter and generally enough of them. The inhabitants were remarkably kind to us.

I was constantly in the country with the wagons. We went out by turns and had no one to control us. Our duty was to load the wagons with hay, corn, meal, or whatever and to keep them company till they arrived safely at the commissary's. From there the supplies were carried in other wagons under other guards to Valley Forge.

Our duty was hard but not altogether unpleasant. I had to travel far and near, in cold and in storms, by day and by night, and at all times I ran the risk of abuse, if not injury, from the inhabitants while plundering them of their property. I could not, while in the very act of taking their cattle, hay, corn, and grain from them, consider this a whit better than plundering—sheer privateering.

But the time came when we were obliged to go back to camp at Milltown for good, whether we chose to or not. About the last of April we were relieved by a party of southern troops.

We accordingly marched off and arrived at camp the next day, much to the seeming satisfaction of our old messmates, and as much to the dissatisfaction of ourselves. At least, it was so with me, for thus far Dame Fortune had been kind. Now Miss Fortune was coming in for her set in the reel. I had returned to my old system of starving. There was nothing now to eat.

Soon we went from camp. We marched toward Philadelphia with three thousand men under the command of young General Lafayette. Arriving at Barren Hill, about twelve miles from Philadelphia, I was placed on guard to protect the horses. At dawn we found the British had advanced upon us in our rear. How they got there was a mystery, but there they were.

Our commander thought the enemy was too strong to be engaged. He ordered a retreat to the Schuylkill River, which we crossed in good order. The British turned their faces away from us and set off for Philadelphia. In a few days we heard that they had left the city and were proceeding to New York. We marched immediately in pursuit. We passed through Princeton and encamped in the open fields for the night, the canopy of heaven for our tent.

In Pursuit of the Enemy

The next morning we came up with the rear of the British army. We followed the enemy for several days, arriving at their camping ground within an hour after their departure from it. Our orders were to give the enemy time to advance, not to attack them unless in self-defense.

We had ample opportunity to see the devastation they made in their rout. Cattle killed and lying in the fields. Household furniture hacked to pieces. Wells filled up. Tools destroyed. Such conduct did not give the Americans any more agreeable feelings toward them than they had entertained before.

It was extremely hot. We kept close to the rear of the British army. Deserters were almost hourly coming over to us.

The officer who commanded my platoon said, "You have been wishing for some days to come with the British. You have been wanting to fight. Now you shall have fighting enough before night."

After all things were put in order, we marched. We heard reports of cannon ahead, but then received orders to retreat! Grating as this was, we were obliged to comply. We had not retreated

THE COMMANDER IN CHIEF, GENERAL WASHINGTON HIMSELF, TOOK AN
OBSERVATION OF THE ADVANCING ENEMY.

far before we came to a muddy creek, where our platoon sat down to rest.

While we sat we saw the commander in chief, General Washington himself, cross the road nearby. After passing us, he rode to a field and took an observation of the advancing enemy. He remained there upon his old English charger while the shot from the British artillery were rending up the earth around him. After he had taken a view of the enemy, he returned and ordered our two Connecticut brigades to make a stand at a fence to keep the enemy in check while the artillery and other troops crossed the creek.

Our detachment formed directly in front of the artillery, as a covering party. We were so far below the hill that the cannon could play over our heads. Here we waited the approach of the enemy, should he see fit to attack us.

The British planted their cannon and began a violent attack upon us. Neither side could easily be routed. The cannonade continued for some time until the British pieces were mostly disabled. The enemy reluctantly crawled back and hid themselves.

We marched toward the enemy's right wing, in

an orchard, and kept concealed as long as possible by staying behind bushes. When we could no longer hide, we marched into the open fields and formed our line. The British retreated to the main body of their army. We pursued. Passing through the orchard, I saw a number of the enemy lying under the trees, killed by our cannon.

We overtook the British just as they entered a meadow. I singled out a man and took aim directly between his shoulders. He was a good mark, being a broad-shouldered fellow. What became of him, I know not. The fire and smoke hid him from my sight. One thing I know: I took as deliberate aim at him as ever I did any game in my life. But after all, I hope I did not kill him—although I intended to at the time.

Our commander shouted, "Come, my boys, reload your pieces, and we will give them a set-off." We did, and gave them a parting salute. The firing on both sides ceased. We laid ourselves under the fences and bushes to take breath, for we had need of it. Fighting is hot work in cool weather, how much more so in such weather as it was on the twenty-eighth of June 1778.

Easy Marches

The next day we marched for Hudson's River. We marched by "easy marches"; that is, we struck our tents at three o'clock in the morning, marched ten miles, and encamped. Every third day we rested all day.

Each brigade furnished its own ferryman to cross the river. I was the ferryman from our brigade. We were suffering for provisions. Near the last trip that I was ferrying, a large sturgeon (a fish in which this river abounds) seven feet in length sprang into our boat. We landed our prize and ordered our messmates to cook it. My share was boiled in salt and water. I fell to and ate a pound and a half, for I was as hungry as a vulture and as empty as a blown bladder.

One day we took a ramble on an old battlefield from the year '76. We saw a number of graves of those who fell in that battle. Some bodies had been so slightly buried that dogs or hogs had been able to dig them out of the ground. The skulls, bones, and hair were scattered about.

Here were Hessian skulls as thick as a bomb-shell. Poor fellows! They were left unburied in a foreign land, with no near and dear friends to lament their sad destiny. But they should have

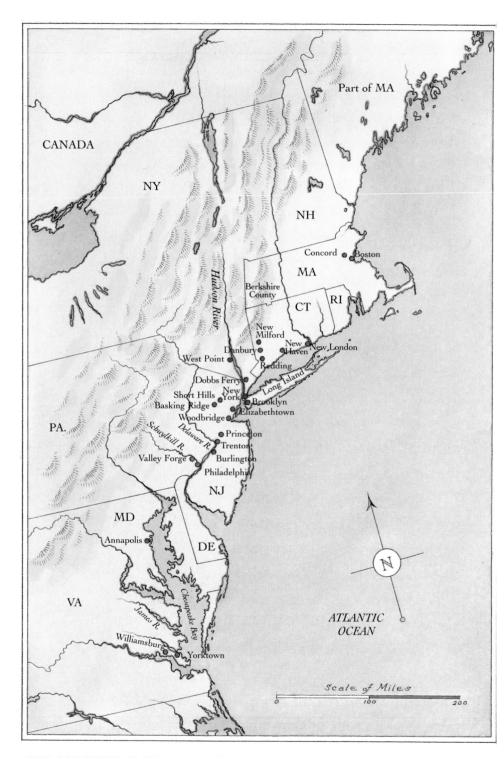

THE COLONIES: FROM NEW ENGLAND TO YORKTOWN

kept at home. We would never have gone after them to kill in their own country. But they were forced to come and be killed here, forced by their rulers who have absolute power of life and death over their subjects. Be careful, you, dear reader: do not allow yourself ever to be brought to such a condition.

I Am Shot at by Americans

Late in the autumn, the main army lay at New Milford, Connecticut. There I nearly obtained a final discharge from the army.

I had been at a small brook to wash my clothes. Among my things was a handkerchief which I laid upon a stone and forgot to take with me. Missing it after roll call I went to get it. It was almost dark before I found it.

I did not hurry back to camp. Suddenly some-body challenged me with, "Who comes there?" I had no idea I was the person being hailed so I kept going. I received a second and a third invitation to declare myself. Still I paid no attention. But our patrols were out and the next compliment I received was a shot. The ball passed very near me.

Instantly I had another salute. I put my best foot foremost. The patrol of fifteen men all had a hack at me. One ball passed near enough to my head to cause my ear to ring.

I sprang for dear life. I was light of foot but had not made many leaps before I ran my knee with all my force against a stump. I went heels over head. I hardly knew whether I was dead or alive. I got up and blundered on till I reached my tent. My knee was in a fine pickle—it swelled as big as my head. When I was questioned about it, I said I fell down, and thus told the truth.

Winter Quarters Again

We arrived at Redding, Connecticut, about Christmas and built huts for our winter quarters. Now came the time between grass and hay, the winter campaign of starving. We struck up fires and lay down to rest our weary bones—all but our jawbones as they had nothing to weary them. We got our huts into such a state of readiness that we moved into them about New Year's Day.

As I have got into winter quarters again, I will here bring my third campaign to a close.

The Campaign of 1779

In February I obtained a furlough to go home. I started from camp intending to go the whole thirty miles at once. I had not a mouthful of anything to eat or carry with me and had only three shillings of old Continental money, worth about as much as its weight in rags. The hopes of soon seeing my friends and the expectation of filling my belly buoyed my spirits.

I arrived at my good old grandsire's at nine o'clock the next morning. I believe the old people were glad to see me. I had an opportunity to see the place of my boyhood, to visit old friends, and to ramble over my old haunts. My time was short so I had to employ every minute to the best advantage.

I remained at home till my furlough had fully expired. The day before I intended to set off for the army, my lieutenant arrived to spend a week

Continental Money

When the colonists declared their independence, there was no United States money. The colonists had been using British pounds, shillings, and pence to buy things. The Continental Congress created Continental money for the new country to use. Unfortunately, the money lost its value. Many Americans found it difficult to pay their bills with the currency. By 1781 it took 225 Continental paper dollars to buy one silver dollar coin.

with his family. He told me I might stay longer and accompany him back to camp. He would be responsible for me. So I remained another week at home.

Mischief in New London, Connecticut

I had not been back at camp for more than a week before I was sent to New London to guard the town. We went by easy marches. Once there, we almost starved to death, and we would have, had we not found some clams.

Just before we left, a privateer brig arrived from a cruise. I went aboard and in the bread room found one bushel of sea biscuits. I filled my knapsack, which was a relief to my hungry stomach. But this bread had nearly as much flesh as bread, being full of worms. It required a deal of circumspection in eating it. However, it was better than snowballs.

We took up our quarters in some old barracks. There were a number of bombshells and damaged wagon wheels lying near. One day we began to contrive some mischief. Five of us carried a wagon wheel up a hill. Then we gave the wheel the liberty to shift for itself and find its own way back down. It took a course directly for the barracks where the men were. We could hear them laughing and talking. Ah, me! What would I not have given had I never meddled with the ugly wheel. It was too late to repent. The barracks were only a single board thick. The wheel would go through it and the men.

We stood breathless. When the wheel was within fifteen feet of the barracks and flying with the motion of a cannonball, it struck something. It sailed thirty feet into the air and over the barracks.

I resolved not to seek such mischief again.

The "Hard Winter"

We lay the rest of the season in New York, across the Hudson from West Point, where we built two strong bombproof redoubts. We remained till December, when we crossed the Hudson and proceeded into New Jersey for winter quarters.

It was cold and snowy. We marched all day and at night took up lodgings in some woods. After shoveling away the snow, we pitched four tents facing each other with a fire in the center. Sometimes we would get an armful of straw to lie upon, which was a luxury. Provisions as usual took up a small part of our time, though much of our thoughts.

We arrived at our wintering ground near Basking Ridge, New Jersey, at the end of December and once more, like wild animals, began to make a city for habitations. We had to level the ground to set our huts upon. We dug out a number of toads, which hopped off as lively as in summertime.

WE GOT INTO OUR HUTS AT THE BEGINNING OF THE NEW YEAR,
WHEN THE WEATHER BECAME INTENSELY COLD.

We built the huts in this manner: four huts in front and two in the rear with a space of eight feet, then four more huts. We had a street fifteen feet wide the whole length. The huts were twelve by fifteen feet. Each had a chimney of sticks and clay.

We got into our huts at the beginning of the new year, when the weather became intensely cold. This is what was termed the "Hard Winter." Hard it was to the poor soldiers. Happy should I have thought myself if that had ended the war. However, I had to see more trouble before that day arrived.

Here I close my campaign of 1779.

The Campaign of 1780

Trying Times

The winter of 1779–1780 was very severe.
The Revolution has been styled "the times that
tried men's souls." I found those times not only
tried men's souls, but their bodies, too. I know
they did mine.

The weather in January was cold enough to
cut a man in two. There were several severe
snowstorms. It snowed for four days and there
fell nearly as many feet deep of snow. I declare I
did not put a single morsel in my mouth for
those four days, except a little black birch bark
which I gnawed off a stick. Several men roasted
their shoes and ate them. Some officers killed
and ate a favorite dog.

Our duty winter and spring was thus: I
marched at eight o'clock in the morning for ten
miles to relieve the guard at Woodbridge. I stayed
there two days and nights. Then I was relieved

and marched to Elizabethtown. Thus it was the whole time we lay here. It was Woodbridge and Elizabethtown. Elizabethtown and Woodbridge. I was absolutely sick of hearing the names.

We were in camp when the "dark day" happened. It grew so dark the fowls went to their roosts, the cocks crowed, and the whippoorwills sang their serenade. People had to light candles in their houses. The night was as uncommonly dark as the day was.

"∂ark ∂ay"
The "dark day" that Joseph Plumb Martin experienced was caused by a solar eclipse.

Our Army Revolts

Winter passed into spring and still we got little to eat. By May the men were exasperated beyond endurance. They saw no alternative but to starve to death or break up the army, give it all up and go home.

This was a hard matter for the soldiers to think on. They were truly patriotic. They loved their country. They had already suffered everything short of death in its cause. Now, after such extreme hardships to give it all up was too much.

But to starve to death was too much also. What was to be done? Here was the army, starved and naked. There was their country, sitting still and expecting the army to do notable things.

One day the men spent their time on the parade grounds growling like soreheaded dogs. At evening roll call they showed their dissatisfaction by snapping at the officers and acting contrary to their orders. One man stamped the butt of his musket upon the ground and called out, "Who will parade with me?" My whole regiment fell in. Another regiment joined us.

We gave directions to the drummers to give signals to us. At the first signal, we shouldered our arms. At the second we faced. At the third we marched to join two regiments camped nearby. We went off with music playing.

One man called out, "Halt in front." The officers seized him like wolves on a sheep and dragged him out of the ranks. We pointed our bayonets at their breasts as thick as teeth, and they let him go.

Colonel Stewart of Pennsylvania questioned us as to why we were behaving thus. We expressed our complaints. He said, "You have won immortal honor to yourselves this winter past by your patience and bravery. Now you are shaking it at your heels. I will see your officers and talk to them myself."

Our stir did us good in the end, for we had provisions directly after, so we had no great cause for complaint for some time.

I Fly

In June we encamped at Short Hills. I was one day on camp guard duty. To defend ourselves from the night dew, we laid down under some trees that stood at the brink of a very deep gully. We took it into our heads to divert ourselves by climbing these trees as high as they would bear us, then swinging off our feet. Our weight would bring us by a gentle flight to the ground.

I determined to have one capital swing. I climbed the tallest tree and swung over the gully. When the tree bent to the horizontal position, it snapped off as short as a pipestem. I was forty feet off the ground and fell feet foremost in quick time. Luckily, the ground was soft, so it did me but little hurt. But I held the broken tree in my grasp and I brought it on top of my unthinking skull. I was knocked as stiff as a ringbolt. I had a severe headache for several days, a memento to keep on the ground and not attempt to act the part of a flying squirrel.

I Join the Sappers and Miners

In July there was a change in my circumstances that was much in my favor. There was a small corps, called Sappers and Miners, whose duty was to build fortifications. I was transferred to this corps and bid farewell forever to my old comrades.

I was appointed a sergeant, as high an office as I ever obtained in the army. I had some doubts in my own mind. But I did use my abilities to perform my duties to my best knowledge and judgment.

We marched to Dobbs Ferry on the Hudson River, where most of the artillery was. Here we lay till the close of the campaign. We built a strong blockhouse near the ferry. One night, a British brig came down the river. Our men discharged several shots at her as she passed the blockhouse. The next day it was reported that General Benedict Arnold had deserted. Unknown to us, he had been aboard that brig.

Benedict Arnold

At the beginning of the War of Independence, Benedict Arnold was one of the best generals in the American army. He helped build the army, was a trusted friend of General Washington, and won several major battles, most notably at Ticonderoga and Crown Point. But, when offered money by the British to sell them the plans for the fort at West Point, New York, Benedict Arnold turned traitor. His scheme was discovered and he fled to England. The British rewarded him with the rank of Provincial Brigadier General and 6,315 British pounds. The rest of Arnold's life was lived in disgrace for he was hated by Americans and distrusted by the very British who paid him.

Had I possessed the power of foreknowledge, I might twice have put Arnold to sleep and saved my country much trouble and disgrace. The first time was in a barn where I was on guard. Arnold ordered me out of the barn so he could sleep.

Had I known what plans he had in his head, I should have had a reckoning with him.

The other time was four days before his desertion. I met him on the road near Dobbs Ferry. He was taking observations and examining the roads. I thought it strange to see him quite alone in such a lonely place. It only wanted a musket ball to have driven him out. I had been acquainted with Arnold from my childhood and never had too good an opinion of him for he was conceited and arrogant.

We lay at Dobbs Ferry till the latter part of October when we went to West Point for winter quarters. We arrived in safety and set to work to build new barracks. We had to go six miles down the river and there hew timber. We carried it on our shoulders from the woods to the river's edge and then rafted it to West Point. By New Year's the barracks were ready to receive us. Till then we had lived in the old barracks, where there were rats enough, had they been men, to garrison twenty West Points.

Our barracks being completed and we safely stowed away in them, I shall here conclude the campaign of 1780.

The Campaign of 1781

I Return Home Again

Nothing material occurred to me till the month of February. I applied to my captain for a furlough so I might visit home, for I saw no likelihood the war would ever end.

I spent my time as agreeably as possible among my friends and family. For ten days I did enjoy myself as agreeably as ever I did in the same space of time in my life. Then I had to return to camp. I confess I never left my home with so much regret before. I need not tell the reason. Perhaps the reader can guess.

My Corps Leaves Me

Upon my return to West Point I found our men all gone and not a soul to tell me where. What to do, I knew not. I had a great mind to set off home again. Then I was informed my group

General Lafayette

The Marquis de Lafayette, a French noble-
man, was nineteen in 1776 when he left
France to fight in the cause of freedom. He
asked for no pay and did not seek a command. He wanted only to serve as a soldier.
He met General Washington and immediately became one of the commander in
chief's closest friends. Their friendship
lasted until Washington died. Lafayette's
presence helped the Americans immensely,
giving them hope that the French might
join the war on their side against the
British. This they eventually did. It was the
French fleet that helped Washington defeat
Lord Cornwallis at Yorktown, the last
major battle of the war.

had gone to Virginia with General Lafayette. I
was thunderstruck. I set off on the journey alone,
not expecting to find the men for hundreds of
miles.

But find them I did, in Annapolis, Maryland.

And they were trying to return to West Point! They were on vessels in the Chesapeake Bay blocked in by British ships. We escaped in our little fleet by sweeping out of the bay on a dark night. Then we made our way back to West Point, where we stayed until the end of May.

I Am Almost Killed Twice in One Day

Our Sappers and Miners were ordered to New York, ahead of the army, in order to make preparations for a siege of the city. When we arrived we halted near a British redoubt. There our officers gave us leave to skirmish with small parties of British horsemen and footmen who were patrolling the fort. I saw four men on their horses. They halloed to me. We became quite sociable. They asked what execution their cannon had just done. I told them they had wounded a dog.

While carrying on this polite conversation I saw the flash of a gun. I instinctively dropped as quick as a loon could dive. The ball passed over me and lodged in a tree. My comrades saw the upper part of my gun drop as I fell and said, "They have killed him."

They were mistaken. The British were mistaken too for they shouted, thinking they had done the job for one poor Yankee. I rose up and slapped my backsides to them as I slowly moved off. I do not know I ever ran a greater risk for my life while I was in the army. "A miss is as good as a mile!" I shouted. However, I know it is poor business to stand thus a single mark.

That same afternoon I almost picked up another of the enemy's shots. While I was talking with a man, an enemy soldier crept up and fired at us. The ball passed between our noses. The gunman walked off but not before we sent something to quicken his pace.

I Meet an Old Friend

One day our Sappers and Miners were ordered to go to a certain place and told that if we did not see or hear the enemy, we were to return.

We had just entered a wood when we found ourselves flanked by thirty enemy. They gave us a hearty welcome. We fired back, but they rushed us before we had time to reload. They gave us chase. I was in the rear of the party that had to cross a fence of old posts.

My men crossed the fence in safety, but I blundered and fell over, catching my right foot where a tree had split from a stump. I hung as fast as though my foot had been in the stocks. I could barely reach the ground with my hands.

The commander of the enemy came to the fence. The first compliment I received was a stroke of his sword across my leg just under the kneepan. It laid the bone bare. Then I realized, I knew him! When we were boys he had been my most familiar playmate. In 1776 he had been a messmate, but he deserted to the enemy. He knew me as well as I knew him. He called me by name and told me to surrender.

I cleared my foot, leaving my shoe behind — and ran till I came to my party. Thus I escaped. This was the only time the enemy drew blood from me during the whole war.

We Lay Siege to Yorktown

In late summer we set out for Virginia. By marches and ships we arrived at the mouth of the James River, where we passed the French fleet. They resembled a swamp of dry pine trees.

After landing we marched to Williamsburg

where we joined General Lafayette. Soon after our whole army arrived. We prepared to move and pay the British, at Yorktown, a visit. Their wish was not to have so many of us come at once. They thought, "The fewer the better." We thought, "The more the merrier." We had come a long way to see them.

We had orders from the commander in chief that if the enemy came out of Yorktown to meet us, we should exchange but one round with them and then decide the conflict with bayonets. The French forces could play their part and we Americans were never backward at trying it. The British, however, did not think fit to give us the opportunity to soil our bayonets in their carcasses.

So we made preparations for laying siege to the enemy. We had holed him. Nothing remained but to dig him out. After taking every precaution to prevent his escape, we settled our guards and brought on our battering pieces and ammunition. On the fifth of October we put our plans into execution.

That night we were ordered to help the engineers lay out trenches. It was a dark and rainy night. A man came alone to us. This stranger inquired what troops we were, talked familiarly with us for a few minutes, and went off. He returned later. By the officers calling him "Your Excellency," we discovered it was General Washington. Had we dared, we might have cautioned him for exposing himself too carelessly to danger at such a time.

The next night we were ordered back to finish the trenches. The troops were ready with shovels but waited to dig until after General Washington had struck a few blows with a pickax so that it might be said, "General Washington with his own hands first broke ground at the siege of Yorktown." The ground was broken. By daylight the men had covered themselves from the danger of the enemy's shot.

As soon as it was day the enemy saw their mistake and began to fire as they ought to have done earlier. Their shot had no effect.

Ours did. The whole number, American and French, was ninety-two cannon. I was in the trenches the day the batteries were first fired. I felt a secret pride swell my heart as I saw our flag raised majestically in the very faces of our foes. A simultaneous discharge of all the guns followed. The French troops shouted, "Huzzah for the Americans!" This was a warm day for the British.

Rush on, Boys!

The siege was carried on warmly for several days until the enemy's guns were silenced. We began our second parallel trench, halfway between our works and theirs. But there were two strong redoubts held by the British that were necessary for us to possess before we could complete our new trench.

At dark we advanced somewhat and lay down to await the signal to attack. The signal was three shells fired from one battery. Our watchword was "Rochambeau," the name of the commander of the French forces. A good watchword, for being pronounced *roSHAMbo*, it sounded, when said quickly, like "Rush on, boys!"

The signal was given by three shells with their fiery trains mounting the air in quick succession. We moved silently to the attack. The enemy discovered us and opened a sharp fire. Many of our shells burst in the ground, making holes sufficient to bury an ox. I thought the British were killing us off in great numbers. One hole happening to

WE REMAINED IN THE TRENCHES TWENTY-FOUR HOURS AND RESTED
FORTY-EIGHT HOURS IN CAMP.

pick me up, I found out the mystery for the slaughter. We were falling into the holes!

Our people cried, "Rush on, boys!" We Miners and Sappers cleared a passage for the infantry, who entered the redoubts rapidly. Our Miners were ordered not to enter, but there was no stopping us. In the heat of the action I saw a British soldier jump over the walls of the redoubt next to the river and go down a bank thirty feet high. When he came to the beach he made off for town, and if he did not make good use of his legs I never saw a man that did.

All of us in the action of storming the redoubts were excused from further duty that night.

None of our men were killed and only eight of the infantry. The second trench was soon finished.

The British Surrender

We remained in the trenches twenty-four hours and rested forty-eight hours in camp. After we had finished the second line of trenches there was but little firing on either side. Lord Cornwallis, the British leader, failed to get out, and he asked for an armistice. On the night of

October 19th the British surrendered. The siege was ended.

The next day we put ourselves in good order to see the British army march out and stack their arms. We paraded on the right-hand side of the road, the French forces on the left. The British appeared, armed, with bayonets fixed, drums beating, and faces lengthening. The Americans and French beat a march as the British passed out between us. It was a noble sight as it seemed to promise a speedy conclusion to the war.

Our army separated then. The French remained where they were and the Americans marched for the Hudson River.

We went into winter quarters in Burlington, New Jersey, some twenty miles above Philadelphia on the Delaware River, where we were quartered in the elegant house that had been the British governor's residence.

Being once more snugly stowed away in winter quarters, this of course ends my sixth campaign.

The Campaign of 1782

Yellow Fever

We had not much to disturb us now, the arm of
British power in America being dislocated by the
capture of Lord Cornwallis. Our duty was not
hard, but I was a soldier yet and had to submit to
soldier's rules and discipline, and soldier's fare.

In January two men were taken down with
yellow fever. One recovered. The other died.
I, too, was attacked with it. The fever took hold
of me in good earnest. I bled violently at the
nose and was so reduced in flesh and strength I
was as helpless as an infant. O! I suffered. Our
officers made a hospital in a house. As soon as
men fell sick they were lodged there.

Gradually I began to mend and recovered what
little reason I ever possessed, of which I had been
deprived from the first attack of the fever. We
were under the care of a local physician. To his
efforts, under Providence, I owed my life.

Likewise, a widow woman helped us. She, pitying angel, every evening sent us a brass kettle of posset—a mixture of wine, water, and sugar—and crackers. O, it was delicious. I never knew who she was. Heaven bless her pious soul.

My hair came off my head. I was as bald as an eagle. It was a grievous sickness, the sorest I had ever undergone. I had never thought myself so near death as I did then.

We Build

Toward the end of summer we went to Constitution Island, opposite West Point on the Hudson River. We blasted rocks to repair works there. The engineers kept us busy.

After we ended our stone blasting, we built new barracks. Elegant ones, too. They were two stories high with wings at each end, brick chimneys, and an upper room large enough to hold two regiments.

In November I was sent downriver to cut wood for our winter's use. We continued at this until Christmas. Now, having provided our wood for the winter, built our barracks, stowed ourselves away snugly in them, and winter having handsomely set in, I will, of course, bring my seventh campaign to a close.

The Campaign of 1783

The War Is Won!

Winter set in early, and not over gentle. We suffered for eatables. I lived half the year upon tripe and cowheels, and the other half on what I could get. We always had short carnivals, but lengthy fasts.

One evening, in the first part of winter, there happened the most brilliant and remarkable exhibition of the aurora borealis, or northern lights, I ever witnessed.

We passed this winter as contentedly as we could, under the hope the war was nearly over. That hope buoyed us up under many difficulties.

Time thus passed until the nineteenth of April, when we had general orders read. The war was over! The prize won for which we had been contending through eight tedious years.

I Leave the Army with a Heavy Heart

On the eleventh day of June 1783, our captain came into our room with his hands full of papers. He ordered us to empty our cartridge boxes upon the floor. This was the last order he ever gave us.

I confess that my anticipation of the happiness I should experience on this day was not realized. There was as much sorrow as joy. We had lived together as a family of brothers for years. We had shared squabbles, hardships, dangers, and sufferings. We had sympathized with each other in trouble and sickness. Now we were to part forever as though a grave lay between us.

I bid a final farewell to the army. I worked at farming that summer and in the fall agreed to teach school near West Point. I had thirty pupils and probably gave them satisfaction. If I did not, it was all one. I never heard anything to the contrary.

In the spring I set my face eastward and did not halt until I arrived in Maine in 1784, where I have remained ever since. At last I rested my war-worn weary limbs.

Here I will make an end to my narrative. Now, kind reader, I bid you a cordial and long farewell.

EDITORS' NOTE

In editing Martin's journal we have kept two goals foremost in mind: faithfulness to his text and accessibility for our reader. We based our book on Martin's original, *A Narrative of Some of the Adventures, Dangers and Sufferings of a Revolutionary War Soldier, Written by Himself*, published in 1830. We shortened his text but otherwise have remained true to his unique way of saying things, altering only where we felt the reader might become confused. Many of his sentences were lengthy. These we shortened for ease of understanding. We also modernized his spelling and punctuation. (The use of brackets indicates, of course, our additions; the parenthetical material is Martin's.) Throughout the book, however, we essentially remained true to Martin's own words.

Joseph Plumb Martin's narrative is a primary source. Primary sources are written documents, images, and artifacts from a particular period of history. Written documents include diaries, letters, wills, and eyewitness accounts. Martin's diary not only helps readers understand the Revolutionary War period, but also gives us a vivid and immediate glimpse into the feelings and thoughts of a person who lived in a different time from our own.

Research for this book was conducted on site at the following places: Yorktown Battlefield, Yorktown, Virginia; Valley Forge National Park, Valley Forge, Pennsylvania; Colonial Williamsburg, Williamsburg, Virginia; Independence Hall, Philadelphia, Pennsylvania;

Saratoga Battlefield, Saratoga Springs, New York; and, most importantly, the State Historical Society of Wisconsin in Madison, Wisconsin, where we were kindly given access to Martin's well-worn volume.

GLOSSARY

baggage train   supply wagons that trailed behind the marching army

battery   an emplacement for a cannon

blockhouse   a strong building made of wooden timbers or logs, with holes in the walls to shoot weapons from

brig   a sailing ship with square sails on two masts

brigade   a large part of an army

commissary   a storage place for an army's supplies

corps (KOR)   a group of soldiers with a special duty; for example, a corps of engineers builds buildings

dilatory   slow

dysentery   diarrhea

extol   to praise highly

field piece   a cannon

fortnight   two weeks or fourteen days

furlough (FUR low)   a leave of absence granted to a soldier

gill   a unit of measure equal to ½ cup

grandsire   grandfather

grapeshot   a cluster of small iron balls fired at one time from a cannon

infantry   soldiers who fight on foot

mortar   a short cannon with a wide mouth for throwing cannonballs at high angles

muster to bring or call together (assemble); a muster day was one on which the militia assembled

outpost a group of soldiers dispatched from the main body of troops to protect against surprise attacks

quartermaster the officer in charge of gathering and distributing an army's supplies

redoubt (ree DOUT) a small earth and wood fort anchoring an army's defensive position

reel a dance

rod a measure of distance; one rod equals 5.5 yards

scapegoat a person who carries the blame for others

stores an army's supplies

tripe the stomach walls of ox and other grazing animals used for food

victuals (VIH tuls) supplies of food

works buildings or structures such as forts, earthen barricades, and trenches; also, structures built by engineers such as docks and bridges

TO LEARN MORE ABOUT THE AMERICAN REVOLUTION

NONFICTION BOOKS

Brenner, Barbara. *If You Were There in 1776*. New York: Simon and Schuster, 1994.

Carter, Alden R. *The American Revolution*. New York: Franklin Watts, 1992.

Collier, Christopher, and James Lincoln Collier. *The American Revolution, 1763–1783*. New York: Marshall Cavendish, 1998.

Egger-Bovet, Howard, and Marlene Smith-Baranzini. *Book of the American Revolution: A Brown Paper School USKids History Book*. Boston: Little, Brown, 1994.

Peacock, Louise. *Crossing the Delaware: A History in Many Voices*. New York: Atheneum, 1998.

Smith, Carter, ed. *Daily Life: A Sourcebook on Colonial America*. Brookfield, CT: The Library of Congress/ Millbrook, 1991.

Zienert, Karen. *Those Remarkable Women of the American Revolution*. Brookfield, CT: Millbrook, 1996.

HISTORICAL FICTION

Avi. *The Fighting Ground*. New York: Lippincott, 1984.

Collier, Christopher, and James Lincoln Collier. *My Brother Sam Is Dead*. New York: Scholastic, 1974.

O'Dell, Scott. *Sarah Bishop*. Boston, MA: Houghton Mifflin, 1980.

VIDEOS

The Revolutionary War. Dan Dalton Productions, 1993.

PLACES TO VISIT

Boston National Historical Park, The Freedom Trail,
    Boston, Massachusetts
Colonial National Historic Park, Yorktown, Virginia
Colonial Williamsburg, Williamsburg, Virginia
Concord, Massachusetts
Independence Hall, Philadelphia, Pennsylvania
Jamestown Settlement, Jamestown, Virginia
Lexington, Massachusetts
Saratoga National Historic Park, Saratoga Springs,
    New York
Valley Forge National Historical Park, Valley Forge,
    Pennsylvania
Yorktown Battlefield, Yorktown, Virginia
Yorktown Victory Center, Yorktown, Virginia

WEBSITES *

Colonial Williamsburg
www.history.org
    Information about Colonial Williamsburg, maps,
    and activities

The Freedom Trail, Boston
www.nps.gov/bost/ftrail.htm

Includes such sites as Paul Revere's house

National Park Service
www.nps.gov/
Information on all National Parks and National
Historical Parks with maps and activities

www.UShistory.org
Information about various historical sites

*Websites change from time to time. For additional on-line
information, check with the media specialist at your local library.

INDEX

Page numbers for illustrations are in boldface.

JB MARTIN M
MARTIN, JOSEPH PLUMB

01